A Three Legged Dog Walked Into a Bar---

Three Legged Dog Walked Into a Bar---

By
Don Carson and Otto Schafer

ISBN 978-0-557-41461-1

Published by Lulu.com

Printed in the United States of America

To all of the Linda's and Bridgette's of the world who for so many years have put up with husbands who think they are great joke tellers.

To Uncle George

Author's Notes

Following is a collection of the best jokes that could be remembered from a lifetime of listening to and telling jokes by two of the most improbable friends you could imagine; Don Carson, a lifelong Southerner born and raised in Georgia and Otto Schafer, a second generation German from New York. Both, in addition to a love of jokes, also have had a lifelong love affair with woodworking, especially carving and scroll saw work.

While they only lived a few miles apart in Cary, North Carolina, they may never have met if Otto had not taken a drive through the subdivision in which Don lived and saw him sitting just outside his garage cutting out a wooden animal puzzle on his scroll saw. He told his wife Bridgette that he just had to stop a second and meet this man.

The two of them soon began working together in Otto's garage on a variety of woodworking projects and eventually into selling some of those items at various Arts and Crafts shows and Fairs in the area.It also soon became apparent to them that they had a mutual love of jokes and would tell each other jokes every time they worked together or spent time together at one of the fairs. Much too often, once a joke was started, the other could tell the punch line. Finally it was decided that they needed to put down on paper the best of the best of these jokes and stories, so that they would not be lost. That led to the production of this book.

All jokes originate somewhere and some of these may be found at other sources or locations. Many came to Otto from Germany and are translated to English here. Regardless of their origination, we believe all jokes belong to anyone who wants to listen to them and if anyone thinks we have stolen "their" joke, we are sorry they might think so.

With the hundreds of sites and thousands of jokes on the internet, you can be assured it probably has been told somewhere before.

What we are certain of is that after a combined 140 years of exposure to jokes, we have not yet remembered all of the ones that we thought were very funny. We hope you enjoy the ones we did.

During the process of placing all of the jokes we could remember in some sort of logical order a strange phenomenon became apparent. Every joke in the world can be placed in only eight categories. We, therefore, have placed the jokes under those eight listings as follows:

ANIMALS

BARS

BLONDES

OLD FOLKS

REDNECKS

RELIGION

SEX

MISC

Enjoy!!

Don Carson and Otto Schafer

Contents

Animals

A chicken farmer read an advertisement for a "Super Rooster" and ordered one since his egg production was falling off. After the rooster arrived and he turned him loose in the farmyard, it was apparent that he was immediately all business and the farmer was very satisfied that he had made a good business decision.

The next morning when he went outside, the yard was littered with chicken feathers and all the chickens look like they had been mauled. The dogs were under the porch with their tails tucked and the pigs were huddled together moaning. All of the cows in the field were mooing and limping around.

Then he noticed a group of vultures circling the far edge of the pasture. As he walked over he saw the rooster lying flat of his back with his feet in the air. He walked up to him and said" Well, Mr. Super Rooster, it looks like you have screwed yourself to death". The rooster opened one eye and said" Shhhhhh- they're getting closer."

A pig farmer decided that he needed to have his prize sow bred and took her to a farmer's house about 25 miles away that advertised breeding. He loaded her up in his truck, dropped her off that morning and returned late in the day to pick her up. He asked the breeder how he would know if the breeding "took". He was told to check the sow in the morning and if she was in the mud, it did not take and he would have to bring her back for another try. If she was on high ground, out of the mud, then all was well.

He anxiously looked outside the next morning and found his sow in the mud, so he loaded her up in the truck and took her back. The next morning he again found her in the mud and again loaded her up for a third try. The next morning he could not bear to look and asked his wife to check out the window for him. "Is she in the mud?" No! "Is she on the high ground?" No! "Then where is she?" His wife replied, "She's in the truck blowing the horn."

A man came in the bar and told the bartender that he would show him something amazing for a free drink. The bartender said. "Ok, if I can see it first". "No problem," said the man as he pulled a small mouse and a tiny stool and piano from his right coat pocket,

The mouse sat down on the stool and started playing the "Beer Barrel Polka" on the piano. Within a few minutes, a crowd had gathered around the bar to watch the amazing mouse. The bartender told him that he was certainly entitled to any drink he wanted on the house. He was soon served a gin and tonic which he quickly drank and then told the bartender that he could show him something else that was just as amazing for another free drink.

The bartender brought him another gin and tonic and said "If you can top that, it's yours." The man reached in his left pocket and took out a small frog which he placed next to the piano. The mouse then started playing and the frog sang "I Did It My Way" so well that he received a standing ovation from everyone in the bar. The man returned his creatures to his pockets and was about to leave when he was approached by one of the customers who asked him if he would sell him the singing frog. He told him that he could not part with such a talented creature.

The man kept after him and finally convinced him to sell the frog for $1,000 cash. The purchaser left the bar with the frog and a smile on his face. The bartender then asked him why in the world he would sell such a valuable frog. He replied, "It's not to worry. That's just an everyday frog. My mouse is a ventriloquist."

A woman walks into a bar with a duck under her arm. The bartender asks, "Where did you get the pig?" The woman responded, "That's not a pig, it's a duck." He answered, "I was talking to the duck, Lady"

Two friends were on a duck hunting trip and were in the lodge eating breakfast when one told the other, "Man, it is cold out there this morning. I'm going to send Jake out to see if there are any ducks on the pond yet. He calls his retriever over, whispers in his ear and lets him out the door.

The other man laughed and said, "Do you really think that dog is really going to tell you about ducks on the lake?" Sure I do, I have been training him for years and he is the smartest hunting dog you will ever see." In a few minutes the dog returns, goes to his master and barks twice.

"See, he said, there are only two ducks on the pond. Let's wait a while before we go out. His friend scoffed at this information and took a stroll down to the pond. Sure enough there were only two ducks on the pond. Then about an hour later, they sent the dog out again.

When he returned, he had a stick in his mouth and waived it around the room before jumping up on his master's leg and started humping it.

"What the hell does that mean?" He asked his friend. "He said that there is so many freaking ducks on the pond that you can't shake a stick at them. Let's go!"

In the old west a three legged dog kicked open the batwing doors to an old saloon and stepped inside. The room grew quiet and the bartender asked, "What do you want dog?" The dog replied," I'm looking for the man that shot my paw."

A prospector during the California gold rush grew tired of the constant competition from other prospectors for the search for gold and moved far away into the nearby mountains.

After a month of total solitude, he journeyed down to a small town he had spotted to renew his supplies. After stocking up at the local emporium, he went into the town's only saloon to have a beer before he began the return trip.

He had done quite well at his new location and had a tidy sum of gold, so he asked the bartender if there was a local whore house. He was told that there were no women in the town and there had not been any there for several years.

"What do the men do for relief around here then?" he asked. He was told that there was a flock of sheep out on the edge of town and that most of the men just went there went they had the urge. He was repulsed at this idea and went back to his prospecting.

A month later, he returned for supplies and then went to the bar to ask, "Where did you say the sheep were?" He was given directions and after reaching the flock soon relived himself. He then thought, "Why should I travel all this far just to visit a stupid sheep? I'll take one back with me."

He soon roped one and started his return trip through town. As he neared the saloon, the men that were out on the street all yelled and ran inside the closest building they could find. He stopped and went inside the saloon. Everyone shied away from him and he asked the bartender what was wrong. "Fella," he said, you have got to be crazy, dragging the sheriff's girl friend through town on a rope like that."

A cowboy decided that it would be fun to take ventriloquist lessons and soon became very adept at throwing his voice. He spent many lonely hours tending to the cattle and often practiced with them. One day he encountered a lone Indian moving his small herd of sheep to a mountain pasture and decided he would have a little fun with him.

He looked down at the Indian's dog and said "What was it that your dog just said?" "Dog no talk!" the Indian responded. The dog then said, "Yes, I can. I was just not in the mood to talk til now.

Then the cowboy looked at the Indian's horse and said "How are you doing horse?" The Indian said "Horse no talk!" The horse said, "Yes I can and I am doing very well sir. Thanks for asking." Then the cowboy looked at one of the sheep and said, "How about you sheep, how are things with you?" The Indian said "Sheep Lie!"

A farmer had a white cow and a brown cow that he wanted bred so he borrowed a neighbor's bull for a few days. He had just put the bull in the pasture when the local pastor came for a visit. He told his son to watch the bull and to come let him know if anything happened. He then ushered the pastor inside for a cup of coffee. While they were talking at the kitchen table, his son burst into the room and shouted, "Dad, the bull just screwed the brown cow." He excused himself and quickly took his son out the back door. "Son, you can't talk that way while the pastor's here."

"Now get back out there and watch the bull. If he does anything just come back and tell me he "surprised" the white cow" In a few minutes, the son returned. His father cut him off before he could say anything and said "Yes, I know, the bull surprised the white cow." The son said, "Boy, he sure did, he screwed the brown cow again."

A cute little girl of about six entered a pet store and told the owner that she wanted to buy a wabbit. He found her lisp very cute and said, "Well, do you want this cute little brown wabbitt with the floppy woppy ears or this white widdle wabbit wight here?" She said, "I don't think my pyfon gonna give too much of a sthit.

An eagle swooped down and caught a small field mouse that he swallowed in one big gulp. As he soared back up, the mouse poked his head out of the eagle's rear, looked down and asked, "Geez, how high are we?" "Oh, about three thousand feet," replied the eagle. "Wow," said the mouse, you wouldn't shit me would you?"

A snail went to a Nissan new car dealership and test drove a new Z-350. He told the salesman he would pay cash for the car if they would change the "Z" logo to an "S". He told him that he had always wanted to go fast and this way everyone would know that a snail was zipping by them. They agreed and a deal was struck.

The next day as he went zooming down the road near the forest where he had grown up, a couple of rabbit friends of his saw him go flying by. One exclaimed, "Man, did you see that "S" car go?"

Two men talking at a bar soon found out that one was a Georgia Tech graduate and the other had attended the University of Georgia. The man from Tech said, "Georgia huh?" I heard you guys would screw anything; horses, cows, mules, dogs, cats, pigs, chickens—The Georgia grad interrupted him and said "Wait a minute, chickens?"

A woman entered an exotic pet store and informed the owner that she was looking for a really unusual al pet. She had tried dogs and cats and birds and that her husband was always complaining that she had no imagination and that everyone had these pets. From her explanations, it was clear to the owner that this husband complained about everything and treated his wife poorly.

He showed her several animals and birds, but nothing struck her fancy. She then passed a cage with the most unusual looking animal she had ever seen and asked about it. It looked like a cross between a Tasmanian Devil and a wolverine. "Oh," the owner replied. "I'm sorry, but he is not for sale. We did not realize when we bought him that he could be a dangerous pet. We call him the Wooly Booger because of his fur coat and disposition. They are trained to attack upon command as protection for their owner and can inflict very serious injuries upon their victims. Let me show you."

He took a large telephone book and threw it on the floor as he opened the Wooly booger's cage. He then said 'Wooly Booger, phone book!" The animal tore into the book and within a few seconds had shredded it into thousands of pieces. He then said "Wooly Booger—cage" and the animal returned to his cage. "I must have him," said the woman.

"Well," replied the owner, "You would have to sign a waiver releasing us from any damage claims and he would cost you $500.00, but why in the world would you want such a dangerous animal?" "I can see it all now. I would take him home and unlock the cage when my husband gets home. He will ask me what in the hell have I got in the cage and I will tell him that it is a Wooly Booger and he will say Wooly Booger—my ass!"

Two rednecks went moose hunting in Canada. They were flown into a remote area by a bush pilot who returned in a week to pick them up. He landed on the lake and taxied up to the isolated cabin where they had been staying to find that both of them had filled their limit with two moose apiece. They were packed and ready to go. He told them he was sorry, but he could only take one moose apiece because of the weight limit for his plane.

They told him that they had the same problem last year and that the pilot had taken out with four moose in the same kind of plane. So he reluctantly loaded the men and the four moose and taxied out on the lake.

He gave the engine full power, but could not clear the tree line and crashed. After the plane finally came to rest, one redneck asked the other, "Where are we?" The other replied "Looks like about the same spot where we crashed last year.

An old farmer had a worn out mule he was trying to sell when he saw his new neighbor, a city dude who had bought the farm next to him to try his hand at farming. The city man had a new John Deere tractor and was trying to plow a very muddy field and had gotten the tractor badly stuck. He walked over to him and told him that it was impossible to plow when the fields were this wet and that the only way he could plow would be with a mule.

He also let him know he had one for sale for $100 and a deal was soon struck. The farmer was paid cash right then and said he would bring the mule over the next morning. When he got up the next day to deliver the mule, he found it dead in the pasture.

He rode over to his neighbor's house and told him the mule had died, but that it was <u>after</u> he had purchased the mule and that he was sorry for his loss.

The city man said, "No problem, keep the money. Just bring the mule on over here and put him by that tree in the pasture." The farmer was taken by surprise but did not want to question his good luck.

He loaded up the mule and placed it near the tree as requested. His curiosity did get the better of him a few days later and he went by his neighbors place to ask him what he had done with the mule. He said, "Well I sold 100 raffle tickets for a mule at 3 dollars each and then after we had the drawing, I told the winner that the mule had died and that I would have to give him back his three dollars. Then I took the $197 profit I made and bought me a good mule."

A mother caught her twelve year old son in the act of masturbating. Hoping to scare him a little so that he would stop this activity, she told him that the stuff that comes out when you do that makes babies so he shouldn't do anything like that until he is married. A young boy of twelve was caught by his mother while

He did stop for several weeks, but the urge got so strong that he went into the woods behind the house and relieved himself. As he was finishing, he had a very large ejaculation that fell to the ground. He decided to cover it up with a large rock so that no one would know. A few days later he had the urge again and returned to the same spot. Before he began, he decided to look under the rock and found a small frog there. He picked it up, cradled it gently in his hands, looked it in the eye and told it, "You are an ugly little booger, but I love you anyway."

A man entered a bar, looked around the room and spotted an attractive woman sitting alone at the bar. He sat down next to her and ordered a drink. In a few minutes, he reached in his coat pocket, pulled out a large green frog and placed him on the bar without saying anything. She asked him what he was doing with the frog. He told her that he was a very special frog and he kept the frog with him at all times to be sure nothing happened to it. She asked what was so special about the frog.

He told her that the frog loved to perform oral sex on women and that he had an extremely large and long tongue. He told her he would show her and took out a bread crumb from his pocket and laid it on the bar. The frog was more than 18 inches away, but had no trouble in flicking out his tongue and retrieving the crumb. He did indeed have a very large tongue.

"Goodness," said the woman. "I would love to try HIM out. He told her that he only lived a little over a block away and that if she was really interested; she could come over and get better acquainted with the frog. She readily agreed and was soon totally naked on his apartment bed as he placed the frog between her legs. "Go ahead frog," he said, but the frog did not move.

He picked the frog up, looked him in the eyes and said, "It's ok, go ahead," and replaced him. Still he did not move, so he picked him up once again and said, "Ok, I'm only going to show you this one more time!"

A devout Catholic man went to his priest after his beloved dog had died to ask him if he would hold a mass for his pet. The priest told him that he did not think it would be fitting to hold a mass for an animal in the church of God. He said, "Why don't you try the church down the street. I am told that if you make a donation to the church that they would probably hold any type of service he would want for his dog?"

The man replied, "Do you think that they would hold a nice service if I donated $50,000?"

"My son," the priest said, "Why didn't you tell me that your dog was Catholic?"

A small rural town developed a problem with squirrels. One business noticed sounds from the attic of the store and soon discovered that several squirrels had moved in. They contacted the local extermination company who quickly ran the squirrels out of the attic and repaired the area were they had gotten in. A few days later they were established in another store's attic. Again the extermination company chased away the squirrels and made repairs. A third business called a few days later to have the same process conducted. This time the squirrels moved into the local Baptist church.

The pastor told his congregation that he knew how to handle this problem. He contacted the owner of the local hardware store and with his help trapped the squirrels one by one, baptized them and released them. Now they only return to the church twice a year; on Easter and at Christmas.

(Alternative ending—they moved into a Jewish synagogue. The Rabbi preformed a Bris on one of the squirrels and none of them have been seen since.)

A major in the Foreign Legion was sent to a desert outpost as the new Commandant. Soon after he was established in his new lodgings, he went to his office. His aide there gave him a requisition to sign as his first official act as Commandant. It was for the purchase of a camel. He asked what the camel was for and was told that the men had been complaining about their lack of access to any women and that the least that they could do would be to provide a camel so that the men could find some relief. The new Commandant did not like this idea, but also did not want to alienate all of his troops on the first day of his new job so he approved the request.

A few days later the camel arrived and all of the men and officers signed up for a date and time for use of the camel. The aide brought the "Camel" calendar in to him and asked if he would like a time slot. "Certainly not!" he replied.

After a month on duty at this outpost that was over twenty miles from the nearest town, the Commandant grew a little restless, called his aide in, and asked if there were any available time slots for the camel.

The aide replied, "Yes sir, in fact she is available at 600 pm this evening. "Bring her around then if you would", he said. At 600 the aide brought the camel to the Commandant. He told the aide to hold the camel by its bridle, got a step stool, dropped his pants and proceeded to have his way with the camel.

When he was done, he jumped down from the stool, pulled up his pants and asked proudly, "Is that the way the men do it around here?" The aide said, "Well, no Sir." "They usually just ride it into town and have sex with women."

A wife was in bed when her husband walked in with a sheep at the end of a leash. He said, "Look honey, I wanted you to see the cow I make love to when we can't be together." She said, "George, if you weren't so stupid, you would know that you are holding a sheep, not a cow." "Martha," he replied, "If you weren't so self-centered, you would realize I was talking to the sheep."

A Scotsman and an Englishman had adjacent chicken farms. They both had large chicken houses and they also had a good number of free range chickens.

Between the sale of chickens and eggs and the free range chickens and eggs, they both had very profitable businesses. They normally were on good terms, but one day had a small dispute. They both were out in their fields gathering free range eggs when they both came together at their property line and both saw a clutch of three eggs. The Englishman bent down to pick them up and the Scotsman said, "Hold on there, Charles, I believe those eggs are on my property." "No, they are clearly on my land, Andrew." The eggs were almost exactly on the dividing line of the two properties and after much discussion and sighting down the line between property markers, the debate only grew more heated.

Finally the Scot said, "I'll tell ye what lad, let's settle this as men. I get to poke you as hard as I can and you will have all the time you need to recover and then you can poke me and the winner gets the eggs. How about it? Are ye man enough to fight for your eggs."

No Scotsman has ever gotten the better of me before, so take your best shot," he replied. With that the Scot wound up and hit the Englishman full on the chin knocking him to the ground and into semi consciousness. It took the Englishman several minutes to recover and as he finally stood he said, "Ok Scotsman, stand ready." The Scotsman replied as he began to walk away with a smile on his face, "That's ok laddie, keep the eggs."

Two roaches were eating out of an overturned trash can in a back alley. One of them said, "I think I will go over to the new restaurant they just opened across the street. I'll be back in a while." He was only gone for about fifteen minutes. When he returned, he told the other roach, "Man you should see this place. It is spotless. All new appliances, sparking tile everywhere, stainless steel counters that they wipe down with disinfectants every time they use them. The place is immaculate." The other roach said, "Please Jimmy, not while I am eating."

A Hindu priest, a Rabbi and a lawyer were all traveling together when their car broke down in the middle of the night out in the countryside far away from the nearest town. They saw an old farmhouse nearby and went there for help. The farmer who answered the door and listened to their problem replied, "I would be glad to drive you into town, but there is nothing open this time of night. Why don't I put you up for the night and then I will take you into town for help in the morning?"

They all agreed that this might be the best route to take and thanked the farmer for his generosity. He said, "There is only one small problem. I only have one spare bedroom with two single beds, so two of you can stay there. The third can sleep in the barn. It's not a cold night and I can give you a pillow and a couple of blankets so you should be comfortable out there. There's plenty of fresh new dry hay."

The Hindu priest volunteered to spend the night in the barn so they all retired for the night. After a few minutes, the Hindu knocked on the door to tell them that there was a cow in the barn and that since they were sacred animals in his country that he did not feel comfortable sleeping there. "No problem," said the Rabbi, I will go to the barn." Again they all retired.

Within a few minutes, there was another knock at the door. The Rabbi said "I did not realize that there was a pig in the barn." The lawyer said, "Say no more. I will go to the barn." In a few minutes there was another knock on the door. It was the cow and the pig.

Two friends were out hiking in the mountains when they found an old abandoned mine shaft. It looked very deep so one of them tossed a small stone down the hole to see how long it took to hit bottom, but they heard no sound. So he picked up a larger stone and tried it. Again, there was not a sound. So they drug over a very large rock and tumbled it into the abyss. They listened and listened but did not hear it hit bottom. One of them saw an old railroad tie nearby and said, "Let's toss that down and if we don't hear something, we have found a hole straight to the center of the earth."

It took them several minutes to drag the heavy timber to the hole and tip it in. A few seconds later a goat ran past them and jumped into the hole. "That was weird," said one of the hikers. "I wonder what made him do that." While they were pondering the situation, a man appeared and said, "Say fellows, have you seen a goat around here?"

They told him that they had just seen a goat run up to the mine shaft and jump in. He replied, "Oh, that couldn't be my goat. I had him tied to a railroad timber."

A man and his wife were out Christmas shopping while they were on a tour of Russia hoping to find some unusual presents to take home. It was very cold and the wife said, "George, I think I felt a snowflake." He said, No, Betty, that was a raindrop. I think it's about to rain." She replied, "Well, dear, I just felt a couple more and I am certain that they were snowflakes." Honey Bunch, I'm sorry, but I can feel them too and I assure you that it was raindrops.

Whatever was falling was very light and the argument continued. They finally stopped a stranger walking down the street and asked him if he spoke any English. He said, "Why, Yes, I do. I am known around here as Rudolph the Red. May I be of some help to you?"

George said, "My wife and I are having a little dispute about what is falling from the sky; whether it is raindrops or snowflakes and we would like to have your opinion. "That is easy," said Rudolph. "That is most definitely rain. It is not yet cold enough for snowflakes to be falling." They thanked him for his help and continued on their way. George then said, "See, Rudolph the Red knows rain, dear."

The animals of the Africa had gotten wind of the game of football and decided to try their hand at a game .The zebras agreed to referee. A lion was chosen as captain of one team and a rhino for the other. They then chose teams from the animals that had shown up to play. Once the teams were decided, a coin was tossed and the Lion's team won the toss and elected to receive.

A giraffe kicked off for the Rhino team and booted the ball well past the end zone, so the Lions took over on their twenty yard line. On the first play the Lion handed off to a gazelle that sped around the end and ran for forty yards before a cheetah caught and tackled him. On the next play, a hippo ran interference for a baboon that made his way down to the Rhino ten yard line.

The Lions scored on the next play from scrimmage with a keeper by the lion that followed his two bull elephant guards into the end zone. With only a wildebeest as a kicker, the Lions missed the extra point and led 6 to 0. A poor kick off by the wildebeest gave the ball to the Rhinos at their forty.

On the very first play, the rhino charged up the field, outrunning the slower elephants and hippos and bulling his way over all of the other animals in his path. No one could stop him as ran in for the score. The giraffe easily made the point after and the Rhino's led 7 to 6.

For the remainder of the half the Lions scored with some difficulty on each of their possessions and then were quickly answered by the Rhino who scored every time he was given the ball. At halftime the score stood at Rhinos 42 and Lions 36. The Lions had missed every single extra point.

At the start of the second half, after the Lions had kicked off to the Rhino thirty, the ball was once again given to the Rhino who charged around left end and had run for twenty yards when, he was slammed to the ground in a vicious tackle. Everyone ran over to the Rhino because they could not see who had tackled him so hard.

There was only a single centipede anywhere in the area. The Lion said "YOU made that tackle?" Yes," replied the centipede, "I love football." "Where the hell were you for the first half?" asked the Lion. The centipede said, "I was putting on my shoes!"

Bars

A customer with a terrible lisp comes into a bar and sits down. When the bartender comes over, he asks, "How muth is a martini?" The bartender tells him that all drinks are $8.00. "Whew!" he says, well then how muth is a beer?" "They are $5.00 for drafts and $6.00 for a bottle. "My goodness," he says, "Well then, just let me have a Bud Dwaft." After a while the bartender comes over to check on him and the man says," I just wanted to twank you for not makin any fun of my speech probwem. The bartender who had a very large hump on his back said, "Not a problem. With my afflication, I make it a point not to make fun of other people's problems. "What afwickion?" he says. The bartender replies, "My hump back." "Oh," he replied, that's a hump back? I thought it was your ass; everything else in here is so high."

Two friends are out walking their dogs on a hot summer day. They pass a bar and one man asks the other if he wanted to get a cool one. He said, "I would love one, but they have a sign on the door that says NO PETS." "Just do what I do," he says. "It will be ok". He walks into the bar with his dog and his friend followed right behind him.

They quickly find a seat and a waitress comes over. She says, "I'm sorry sir, but no pets are allowed inside. I'm afraid you will have to take your dog outside."

"He looks at the ceiling and says, "Ma'am, this is my Seeing Eye dog and he takes me everywhere I go. We haven't had any trouble in any other bar around here."

She looked down at the German Sheppard at his feet and said," I am so sorry sir; I didn't realize he was a Seeing Eye dog. Please let me get you a drink on the house." "Fine," he said. I'll have a Bud Lite."

She then turned to the other man and said, "I'm sorry sir, but you WILL have to take your dog outside." "You've made another mistake young lady. This is MY Seeing Eye dog." "A Chihuahua?" she replied. You have a Chihuahua for a Seeing Eye dog? "A Chihuahua!" he shouted. "A Chihuahua! Those bastards gave me a Chihuahua?"

A Scottish man came into a pub in Dublin and ordered three glasses of Guinness. He sat down at a table and slowly drank all three and then ordered three more. This time, the bartender said, "Say fellow, if you're going to have three more, why don't you order them one at a time. They won't get warm on you that way."

"Aye, laddie, ya do nay understand. Me job just got me moved here to Dublin and me two brothers are back in Scotland. We always drink together when I am home. So I drink three because it makes me feel like I am at home with me brothers."

So every day for weeks, the same man would come into the bar and order three beers twice before he left. The one day he came in and only ordered two beers. The bartender feeling badly for the Scot walked over to him and said," I see you're only having two beers tonight."

"Did something bad happen to one of your brothers?" "Nay laddie, me brothers are just fine and drinking every day, it's me that decided to quit drinking.

A drunk leaves a bar and goes straight across the street into a Catholic church and enters a confession box. In a minute, a priest comes to the other side, but the drunk does not say anything. He coughs to let him know he is there, but there is still no response. So he then knocks three times on the confessional wall. The drunk says, "No need to knock buddy, there's no toilet paper over here either.

A man was at a bar alone drinking a vodka martini when a nun came over to him and said, "Sir, don't you know that liquor is the drink of the devil and that you are wasting your life away here drinking these vile drinks when you could be out in the world doing God's work?" He looked at her and said, "Maybe so Sister, but I am not a bad person. I just enjoy the taste of a drink now and then. Tell me have you ever tried a drink? You might enjoy it and just having a drink now and then has never hurt anybody." "Never have the potions of the devil passed my lips and besides how would it look for a nun to be sitting here drinking a drink with you?"

He said, "I'll tell you what, let me order you a vodka martini for you to just try out and I will get the bartender to put it in a teacup for you so that no one will know what you are drinking. "Well, Ok" she said, "Just let me run to the bathroom first". As soon as she left he called the bartender over and ordered another drink for himself and one in a tea cup. The bartender looked at him and said, "It's that nun again isn't it?"

A man who had been drinking at a bar for a while was leaving when the bartender said," Hey pal, you need to pay up". The drunk said, "I already paid you."

The bartender said, Oh, ok, if you say you have then you must have." The drunk walked out and met an old friend on the way in and told him about the bartender.

He told him that the bartender didn't keep up with how much people were drinking and that he didn't have a clue about who had paid. So the second fellow drank all he wanted and got up to leave. The bartender said, "Hey, Mac, you need to pay up" He replied, "I already did!" Oh, well, if you say you did, I guess you did. When the man is leaving he sees someone he knows and tells him all about this sloppy bartender. The third man drinks his fill and gets up to leave.

The bartender tells him," Mac, there have been a couple of people here earlier who got up to leave without paying and claiming that they did, I swear that if one more guy tries that trick tonight, I am going to clean his clock."

The third drunk looks him in the eye and says, "I don't blame you. Now, if you will be so kind as to get me my change, I will be on my way."

A pirate is sitting at a bar. He has a patch over one eye, a hook for a hand and a peg leg. Another customer comes in a sits down beside him. After a while he asks the pirate, "Say, mate if you don't mind my asking; how did you lose your leg?"

He said, "I was drinking a little too much grog out on the high seas one day and fell overboard. Just as they were pulling me back on board, a shark bit me and took off my leg at the knee. "Man, that's terrible. So how did you lose your hand?"

The pirate said, "We were in a mad fight with another ship and just as we were boarding her, a man cut me hand off with his sword."

"Wow," the man said, "You have really had your troubles, so what happened to the eye?" "Oh, I looked up one day and a bird crapped in it. "You mean bird crap caused you to lose your eye?" "Well," the pirate replied. "You see, it was the first day I had me hook."

A very large and burly man who is also quite drunk stands up in the middle of the bar and says, "I can whip any man's ass in this bar." He turns to his left and looks down the bar and says, "All of you on this side are "Assholes" and if you have a problem with that stand up and fight." No one moves. Then he looks down the bar to his right and says, "And all of you on this side are "Bastards" and if you have a problem with that, stand up and fight."

One scrawny fellow get up and walks toward him. The large man says, "So you want to fight do you?" "Oh, No sir," said the scrawny man, I'm just on the wrong side.

Two drunks were at a bar and sat down next to each other in an Irish pub in Shannon, Ireland. One said to the other very loudly, "Say lad, are ye from around here?" "Nay," said the other just as loudly, "I grew up in Dublin." "So did I" said the first man. "I even graduated from St. Mary's high school there." "No foolin", said the other, "So did I." "I lived on James Street there. Where did you live?" You're kidding; I lived on James Street too. A man nearby asked the bartender, "What is with these two yapping so loudly?" "Oh," said the bartender, "Don't mind them. It's just the Murphy twins drunk again.

A man at a bar notices another man who had fallen off his stool and was having a terrible time getting back into it. He went over to him and helped him back onto his perch and said, "Say don't you think you have had a little too much to drink."Have you got a way home?"

"The man replied, "Sure I do, I was just thinking about driving home. I have already had my usual two drinks."

The first man said, "I don't think that would be a good idea. How about I drive you home? You can come get your car tomorrow." The drunk said, "No, I can make it. It's only a few miles." The first man took him by the arm and said, "Not a good idea. Come on, let me take you home. I insist."

He said, "Ok," and promptly fell off the stool when he tried to stand up. It took the stranger about five minutes to get the drunk out the door and into his car. He could barely stand and fell whenever he tried to take a step. He literally had to drag and carry the man to his car. It was only a few miles to the man's house and he then had to repeat the process to get him to his door.

The man's wife opened the door just as they approached and said, "Oh, my goodness, you have brought Charles home. I wasn't expecting him back so soon." "You're welcome ma'am. I just didn't want to see him driving in this condition. "Well, thank you, young man. Now what did you do with his wheel chair?"

A very stout and surly man came into a bar with a pad of paper and a pen in his hand. He walked up to the first man he saw at the bar and said, "What's your name mister?" The man replied, "Jim Johnson, why are you asking?" He wrote the man's name down on his pad and replied, "I making a list of all the people in this bar whose butt I can whip and I have your name down on my list, any problem with that?"

The man shook his head no, so the drunk moved down the bar to the next man and asked his name. "Darwin Johnson" was the reply. "Well, Mr. Johnson," he said, "I'm making a list of everyone in this bar whose ass I can kick and I just wrote your name down on my list. Is there any problem with that?" He was told, "No, sir".

By the time he reached the end of the bar, he had seven names on his list and no one had challenged him to verify his butt whipping abilities. When he reached the last man, he said, "What's your name?" "Bubba Anderson," replied the man. "Well, Bubba," said the drunk, "I am the baddest man in this bar and I am making a list of everybody in here whose ass I can kick.

"So I am writing your name down. You have any problem with that?" The man looked over the very large name taker and said, "You know, I have seen you take names all the way down this bar and it's possible you could have kicked any of those fellow's butts, but I don't think you can kick mine." "You don't huh?" said the drunk. "No! I don't," was the reply. "Well then," he said, let me just take you name off this here list.

Blondes

(Writers note--- Ok, before you get upset, this contains both men and women blond jokes and we even have one where the blond gets the upper hand)

A Brunette went to her doctor to complain that it hurt her everywhere on her body that she touched. She said, "Let me show you." She then touched her arm with her index finger and yelled in agony. She then touched her leg and cried out in pain. "See!" she said. The doctor asked. "You are not really a brunette are you?" "No, I am actually a blonde," she replied. "Why?" "Just wondering," said the doctor, "It looks like to me that you have a broken index finger."

A young blonde decided that she wanted to try out ice fishing. She read everything she could find about the sport and carefully made a list of all of the equipment she would need. She then went to a local sporting goods store and after asking advice on several things completed her list of such items as a good rod and reel, an ice hole saw, a comfortable collapsible chair, a small heater and all of the line, lures, sinkers, etc. on her list.

She decided to try out her luck and got up early with a smile on her face to go "Ice Fishing. As soon as she had deposited all of her equipment on the ice, she unsheathed her ice saw and began trying to cut a hole in the ice.

All of a sudden, she heard a booming voice say, "There are no fish under the ice!" She looked around and could see no one, so after a few minutes she resumed her efforts. Again the voice said" Lady, there are NO fish under the ice!" This time she looked skyward and said, "God, is that you?" The voice answered, "No, this is the skating rink Manager and there are NO fish under the ice."

A blonde was sitting in the window seat on a plane when a young business executive sat down in the aisle seat beside the beautiful young girl. After several attempts to engage her in conversation, it was apparent that she did not want to talk and he was frustrated that he could not seem to gain her interest. He asked her if she would like to play a guessing game. She told him, "Thank you, but I would rather not." He said, "How about I ask you a question and if you can't answer it, you have to give me $5.00."

"Then, you get to ask me a question and if I can't answer it, I will give you $100.00." This got her attention and she agreed to play. He asked her if she knew the capital of Hungary which she did not, so gave him $5.00 from her purse. She then asked him, "What goes up a hill with three legs and comes down with five legs? He was stumped. He made some calls to friends on his cell phone and looked everywhere on his laptop, but could not come up with an answer so he paid her the $100.

She put the money in her purse and said, "I really don't want to play anymore." "He said, "Ok, but you have to tell me what in the world goes up a hill with three legs and comes down with five?" She smiled, opened her purse, said, "I don't know" and gave him $5.00.

A young couple was being kept awake late at night by their neighbor's barking dog. One night it seemed to be incessant and they could not get any sleep. The blonde wife said, "I have had enough of this". She put on her bathrobe and stormed outside. After she returned a few minutes later, her husband said, "The dog is still barking as bad as it did before you went outside"

I know," she replied. "I moved him to our back yard. Let's see how THEY like it."

Three male construction workers, all blond, were working as riveters on a high rise apartment building. When they stopped for lunch one day, one of them opened his lunch sack and said, "My God, it's peanut butter and jelly again. I swear if I get peanut butter and jelly one more time, I am going to jump off this building." The second fellow opened his and said, "Homemade tacos again!" If I get them one more time this week, I'm going to jump off this building.

The third man opened his and said, "Looks like I have got the same problem; bologna for the third time this week. One more time and I am jumping too."

The very next day when the first man opened his lunch sack, he said" Peanut Butter and Jelly! I can't take it anymore and jumped from the building. The second man looked at his and saw Tacos and joined his coworker. The third looked at his and saw a bologna sandwich and also jumped. The wives held a joint funeral where the first wife said, "If I had only known how much he hate Peanut Butter and Jelly sandwiches."

The second wife said, "If I had only known that he didn't want the tacos every day." The third wife said, "I just wish Charles would have let me make his lunch for him."

A very pretty blond girl was taking her final exam in American History at the end of her freshman year in college. It soon became apparent to her that she had not studied enough and was having difficulty with every question even though it was a simple true/ false test. She finally decided that she would do just as well with a coin toss and got a quarter out of her purse. She then answered each question as True for Heads and False for Tails.

The professor noticed what she was doing and decided to just let fate take its course with this student. After everyone else in the room had completed and turned in their tests, he saw that she was still flipping the coin. So He walked over to her and asked if she was about through with the test. She replied, "Oh, I finished with it twenty minutes ago, I'm just checking my answers."

Two blond candidates for jobs on a police force were being tested in an attempt to determine their trainability for the job. The first woman was brought into the exam room and shown a profile of a criminal from their files. She was allowed to study the picture for one full minute and then it was hidden from her view. "Now," said the examiner, "Can you tell me anything you saw about this man that would help identify him?" "Yes," she said, He only has one eye." He replied," It's a profile shot. Can you tell me something else you saw?"

"Yes, He only had one ear." With that the examiner gave up, excused the candidate and invited the next one in. He repeated the same scenario with this blonde, but when he asked if she saw anything that might help in identifying the criminal, she replied, "Yes, He wears contacts." This took the examiner by surprise and his curiosity was aroused, so he excused himself for a minute.

When he came back he told her, "Ma'am, I went back to this man's records and he does indeed wear contacts. Can you tell me how in the world you were able to deduce that fact?" "She said, "It was easy. He only had one ear, so he could not possibly wear glasses."

Miscellaneous

A man was traveling on an old dirt country road when he encountered a long hole full of muddy water. He tried to plow on through, but became hopelessly stuck. He spotted an old farmer out in a pasture near him that had a pair of large oxen. He walked over to his fence and asked him if he could help him get his car out of the mud with his oxen.

He said "Sure, but I will have to charge you $50 for my time. He agreed and within a few minutes the farmer had hitched up his oxen to the car and pulled it free. He paid the farmer and thanked him and as he was about to leave told him, "It sure was lucky for me that you were out here in the field when I got stuck."

The farmer replied, "Yep, you are the ninth car I've pulled out this morning. "Gosh," the man said jokingly. "When do you get your plowing done; at night?" "Nope he said, "That's when I fill up the hole with water."

A young woman was having a terrible time with her garden. Nothing seemed to be growing very well. She noticed that her neighbor's garden was lush and green with flowers and vegetables in profusion. She decided to ask him his secret to such a wonderful garden.

He told her that he firmly believed that a garden responds to its caretaker and that she needed to spend some time in communion with her plants. He suggested dancing in the nude at night in her garden.

She thought this was strange, but decided to try it out and for the next two weeks danced in the nude in her garden in the late evening. Then as she was out in her garden one day, the neighbor asked how things were going.

She said, "Thank you so much for your advice. All my flowers and vegetables seem to be doing a lot better and I don't understand it, but all my cucumbers must be at least twelve inches long."

A redneck was at the barber shop getting his hair cut. The barber asked him if he had heard that the local high school had gotten a car and now was using it for Driver's Education on Mondays through Thursdays. He asked, "Why not on Fridays?" The barber replied, "Oh, that's when they are using it for Sex Education."

A handsome young prince was being pressured by his father, the King, to get married. He wanted to retire and pass on the kingdom to his son, but wanted him to have a wife to serve as the new queen. The prince searched high and low but could not seem to find a suitable mate. Then one day he met a fair young maiden with whom he was immediately enchanted. He wooed her for two weeks and then could stand it no longer and asked her to marry him. She said, "I will marry you if you can tell me the answer to one question and I will give you one month to find the answer." "He replied, "Anything my love, what is the question?" She said, "What is the one thing that all women want?"

The prince asked the question of everyone he knew and sought out every wise man he could find in the kingdom, but no one had the answer. The day before the month was to expire; he came upon a hideous witch who told him that she would give him the answer if he would spend one night with her.

The prince was now so desperate that he agreed to the deal. The witch told him, "The answer is that all women want to be able to make their own choices. You must pay the price agreed upon this very night."

The prince returned to his bride to be and she agreed that this indeed was the correct answer. The wedding was then set for the next day. That night the prince met the witch to pay his debt.

Just as they were to begin making love the witch turned into his beautiful bride to be. After making passionate love, she told him, "I can be a witch during the day and a lovely woman at night or I can be a lovely girl during the day and a witch at night. After we are married tomorrow, you must make the decision of what you want me to do." The prince thought and though about his problem until the wedding was over. He had great trouble in deciding whether he wanted a queen during the day that could be with him at all of the important functions or if he wanted a beautiful woman in his bed at night.

When he was called upon for his answer he said, "I want you to decide which of the two options is the right one for you." She replied, "That was the perfect answer, I will be your beautiful wife ALL of the time.

The moral of this story—Give a woman what she wants or things are going to get ugly.

A very prestigious cardiologist died, and was given a very elaborate funeral by the hospital he worked for most of his life. A huge heart covered in flowers stood behind the casket during the service as all the doctors from the hospital sat in awe. Following the service, the heart opened and the casket was rolled inside. The heart then closed, sealing the doctor in the beautiful heart forever.

At that point, one of the mourning doctors burst into laughter. With everyone in the chapel staring at him, he said, "I am so sorry. I was just thinking of my own funeral. I am a gynecologist. The proctologist fainted.

A man was walking through Wal-Mart calling out "Crisco! Crisco!" One of the employees came over to him and said, "Sir, all of the food products are over on aisles 5, 6, and 7. "Oh," he replied, "I was just trying to find my wife. I call her Crisco when we are out in public." "What do you call her at home?" asked the young man. "Lard Ass", he replied.

The CIA decided that they need to hire a new assassin and had narrowed their search down to three candidates. They brought them all in for a final test. The first is brought into a room and given a gun. He is told that his wife is sitting in the next room and that he must go in there and shoot her. He quickly tells them that he can't do that and is as quickly dismissed as unsuitable for the job at hand. The second candidate is given the same mission.

He enters the room, but soon comes back out and tells them that he just can't shoot his wife. The third candidate is a woman and when she is told that her husband is in the next room and that she must take the gun and go in and shoot him she responds, "No problem."

She enters the room and the three interviewers hear four rapid gunshots and then loud banging and scraping that seemed to go on for forever. She then reenters the room splattered in blood and says." That gun you gave me had blanks in it, so I had to beat him to death with a chair.

Three missionaries are captured by a small band of natives. They are brought to a remote village and tied to trees. The chief soon makes an appearance, walks up to the first man and says "Death or Boola-Boola?"

"Well, I don't know what Boola-Boola is but I certainly don't want to die, so I choose Boola-Boola." He was untied from the tree and then gang raped by all twenty of the male tribe members with the chief going first and last. He was released to slink off into the jungle. He then asks the second man, "Death or Boola-Boola?" He answered, "I don't want to die either. I will take the Boola-Boola." He was untied and given the same treatment and released.

Then the chief asked the third mad, "Death or Boola-Boola?" "I will not suffer the indignation of your Boola-Boola. I choose Death!" "Death?" Asked the chief. "Yes! Death!" replied the missionary. The chief looked puzzled for a minute and then said. "Ok, then it will be Death; Death by Boola Boola!"

A man arrived at the Pearly Gates and was met by St Peter. As he was being checked in, he was asked how he died. He said, "I came home early to my fifth floor apartment to find the elevator not working. After walking up, I found my wife in bed with another man. He jumped out of bed and raced out of the apartment before I could catch him. I chased him down the hall and out a door to a fire escape. I could see him going down the steps, so I grabbed the refrigerator that was at the end of the hall and flipped it over onto the fire escape.

Just as I was shoving it at the man, I guess from the walk up and the lifting of the refrigerator, I had a heart attack and died. Peter said, "Very well my son, you may pass on through"

Shortly thereafter, another man arrived and was asked the same question. "Do you remember how you died?" He said, "Well, I was hiding in this refrigerator—

A man who was having a great deal of pain in his private areas went to see his doctor. He was soon diagnosed with Chinese Syphilis. "What can you do for it," he asked the doctor. He was told, "There is nothing short of amputation of the penis that I can do that will save your life." "My god." He replied. "I think I will get a second opinion before we do that." So he went to another doctor and told him nothing of the visit to the first doctor. He received the same diagnosis and the same treatment option.

He sadly went home dreading this drastic treatment and the life he would be forced to lead after the surgery.

The next day, it came to him that if this was a Chinese disease then why not consult a Chinese doctor to see if there were any other options than amputation possible? He made an appointment with a highly regarded Chinese doctor and after a few tests was told "I'm afraid you have Chinese "sypheriss"; very bad, very bad disease."

The man interrupted, "Yes, I know and the only treatment is amputation of the penis, right? "Oh, No, said the doctor. We no give amputations for this disease. "No?" said the man excitedly. "Oh, no, said the doctor, "Two, three weeks, fall off by itself."

A reporter for the Anderson, SC Herald was walking down the street when he saw a teenager and his younger brother walking up the street toward him. Just then, a large pit bull broke free of the rope that held in a nearby yard and attacked the younger boy. The older boy grabbed a nearby stick, stuck it in the dog's collar, twisted it and soon freed his brother from the death grip the dog had on his leg. Unfortunately, the dog died during this ordeal.

The reporter ran to the boys and said" That was the most heroic thing I have ever seen young man. I can see our headlines tomorrow "Young Tiger Fan Saves Brother from Vicious Dog".

"Well." Said the young man, I'm not exactly a Clemson fan." "Oh," said the reporter, "Ok then we'll change it to read "Gamecock Fan Saves Brother from Vicious Attack.""Sir, the young man said, I'm not a South Carolina fan either.

My allegiance has always been with the Bulldogs of the University of Georgia." Well, in that case, he replied, I guess I will have to change it to "Young Redneck Bastard from Georgia Kills Beloved Family Pet."

A young college graduate applied for a sales position with large superstore telling the manager that he was the "World's Best Salesman" and that he could sell anything. He liked the young man's attitude and told him he would give him a trial week in the camping goods area before he put him on full time. That week the young man tripled sales in that area selling tents, cooking equipment, sleeping bags, etc., until they were out of stock on several items.

He brought him into his office and told him that he was convinced and placed him on a nice salary and commission sales incentive program and assigned him to the Sporting Goods area where sales were lagging.

The boss was interested in the techniques his new hire was using so he hid behind rows of merchandise and watched him waiting on a customer.

He was showing the customer a fish hook and before long the customer had an arm load of fishing lures, line, sinkers and floats.

"Now do you have a good rod and reel?" the customer was asked. When he said "No", he was shown several and picked one out.

In the next few minutes he was sold a creel, a fishing tackle box, a casting rod and some hip waders. Just as the man was about to leave, he told him."You know, if you want to get out there where the big ones are, you need a boat."

He started showing him jon boats and slowly moved him up to more and more expensive boats until the customer finally purchased a fully equipped $20,000 fishing boat. When the customer left, he rushed over and started pumping his salesman's hand. "That was one of the most amazing sales jobs I have ever seen. Imagine a customer walks in looking for a fishhook and walks out with about $21,000 worth of merchandise."

"Well, actually," the young man replied, "he stopped me to ask if I knew where they kept the Tampax in the store," so I said, "Hey, if you are not doing anything this weekend , why don't you go fishing?"

A man with no arms applied for the recently vacated job of bell ringer at a large Catholic church. The priest told the young man that this was a very important job and that the bells had to be rung exactly right for the various services that were held at the church. He asked," How can you do that with no arms?" The young man said "I ring the bells with my face."

"I can get a great feel for exactly how they should be rung that way and have had a great deal of experience at this over the past few years." The priest reluctantly agreed to try him out since they had services later that day. When the bells began to ring from the bell tower, everyone was enthralled. They were rung as never before with sweet melodious tones.

Then, the man slipped and fell to his death in the courtyard. A crowd gathered around the fallen man and someone asked the priest, "Who was he Father?" "I don't know," he replied, "but his face sure rings a bell.

A week later another man applied for the job telling the priest that he was the brother of the man who had died there the previous week. Again he agreed to try out the bell ringer and at the first service was pleasantly surprised at the beautiful notes the man was able to get from the bells. Half way through the service, he slipped and fell to his death. Everyone gathered around the man and the priest was asked who this man was. He said' "I don't know, but he is a dead ringer for his brother."

Three men had been marooned on a deserted island for two years. They were walking along the beach one day when they spotted a lamp that had washed ashore. When one of them picked it up and wiped off the sand, a genie appeared from lamp. The genie said, "Thank you for freeing me from the lamp. As a reward I will grant each of you a wish. The first man said, I am from New York and I miss my old life there more than you can imagine. All I want is to be back home in New York City. The genie waived his hand and POOF! The man was gone.

The second man said, "I feel the same way that Joe did. I am from Southern California and all I want is to be back home in San Diego." Another wave and POOF! , he was gone. The third man said, I am just an old redneck boy from a small poor town in South Georgia and I sure don't want to go back there and start working at the sawmill again, I was just getting to like old Joe and Bill a lot and I sure do miss them. I wish they were back here on the island.

A man and his wife vacationed in Panama City every year and every year as they first went down to the beach, he would take his wife by the open cockpit plane that advertised a half hour ride for two people around the area for $50.00

Every year he tried to get his wife to take the plane ride, but she always refused saying, "Bill, 50 dollars is 50 dollars and we don't need to be wasting our money like that."

This same scenario went on every year until they celebrated their 50th wedding anniversary by taking their usual vacation to Panama City Beach. When they neared the plane, he asked her again as a special favor to celebrate their anniversary. She said once again, "Bill, 50 dollars is 50 dollars. We don't need to be wasting it.

With that the pilot came over and said, "Folks, I've been listening to you for as long as I can remember arguing about this plane ride. As a gift for your anniversary, I would like to take you up for a ride, but I have one condition. I don't want either one of you to say one word. If either one of you talks; it will cost you the 50 dollars. I would like for you both to just enjoy the ride with no arguing, Deal?"

They both agreed and were soon airborne. He took them on a special ride all over the area, out over the ocean, the downtown area and up and down the beach, He even gave them a few loops and spins and hard baking turns to show off the power of the aircraft. When he landed and switched off the engine, he noticed that only old Bill was in the seats behind him.

"Alarmed, he asked, "Where is your wife?" "Oh." He said, "She fell out about 10 minutes ago" "Why didn't you say something," asked the pilot. He replied, "Well, 50 dollars is 50 dollars, you know."

A man had a flat tire and pulled to the curb to change his tire. He got out the jack and positioned it, removed the hubcap and loosened the lug nuts. After raising the tire, he removed the lug nuts and placed them in the hubcap for safekeeping. As he was removing the tire, he stepped on the hubcap and all five of the lug nuts rolled out of the hubcap and down into a nearby drain.

He could see the lug nuts about 5 feet below the steel grate that covered the drain, but could not figure out anyway to get to them. As he was cursing his luck and wondering aloud, what in the world he would do now, a voice said, "I have an idea."

He looked up and could see by a nearby sign that he had parked in front of the local insane asylum. An inmate was looking at him from a second story window and said "Why don't you take one lug nut from each of the other three good tires and use them. That should get you safely back on the road." "What a great idea," said the man. "What in the world is someone with that kind of intelligence doing in a place like that?" He responded, "I'm in here because I'm crazy, not because I'm stupid."

An Avon lady was making her rounds in a downtown skyscraper just before Christmas and had several orders to deliver to customers on some of the upper floors. Just as she entered the elevator alone she had a very abrupt and powerful emission of gas. Since she was traveling to the 20th floor, she was afraid that the elevator would stop along the way and since she was alone, whoever entered would have no doubt about the origination of the pungent atmosphere.

She quickly searched her handbag for any product she might have handy to cover the odor. She found a small aerosol can of pine scent room freshener and sprayed a healthy dose in the confined space.

No sooner had she completed the spraying than the elevator stopped on the 14th floor and a man entered. He wrinkled his nose and coughed. Hoping that she had successfully covered her tracks, she looked the man directly in the eye and said, "Is anything wrong?" He replied, "If I didn't know better, I would say some one has shit a Christmas tree in here."

A Cajun woman shopping in a Wal-Mart went to the Pharmacy area and asked one of the druggists, "Do you have anything to geet reed of bugs in de bush?" Not understanding exactly what she wanted, he directed her to some cans of pesticide which she purchased.

A week later she was back in the store and the druggist asked her if she had gotten rid of the bugs. She said, "Yes, de bugs are all gone, and de hair is all gone from de bush and Pierre, poor Pierre, he's moustache is all gone too."

A man was making his way down a very steep and dangerously curvy mountain road in his convertible sports car. He met a woman coming towards him who rolled down her window and yelled at him, "PIG!". He yelled back as she passed, "BITCH!" He then rounded the next corner and crashed into a large pig in the middle of the road.

A man was staying in a very luxurious hotel in Brussels and was enjoying one of the most elaborate exercise rooms he had ever encountered. As he finished his work out, he needed to go to the bathroom very badly.

The men's room door was open with a "Closed for Cleaning" sign posted. He asked the attendant if there was another restroom nearby.

He was told that since there was no one else there at the time that he could just use the Lady's Restroom. He was told to just lock the door until he was finished and then cautioned not to touch any of the buttons in the restroom since it was designed for women.

As soon as he was seated he noticed four buttons next to the commode. They were marked WW, WA, PP and ATR. His curiosity got the better of him and despite the caution he had been given pushed the WW button, He rear was gently covered with very soothing warm water. He found this very refreshing and decided to push the WA button. A gentle warm breeze of air soon dried off his bottom and he could not wait to push the PP button.

A small powder puff gently applied a small dab of a very sweet smelling powder on his rear. He was so enthralled with these devices that he them pushed the ATR button. The next thing he knew, he awakened in a recovery room at the nearest hospital.

He asked the nurse what had happened and she said, "We figure you must have pushed the ATR button. Sir, that stands for Automatic Tampon Remover. You will find you penis under your pillow."

Soon after his creation Adam spoke to God saying, "Lord, you have provided me the most beautiful place on earth with all the food one could want and beautiful weather. I have dominion over all of the animals of the world and should not want for anything. But, I am lonely and I have been having strange urges. Is there something wrong with me?" "No, Adam," He replied. The feelings you are having are perfectly normal. I need to create a companion for you, so I will make a woman for you." "What is a woman, Lord?" Adam asked.

The Lord replied, "She will be a beautiful creature who will satisfy your cravings whenever you wish, cook all your meals for you and tend to all of the household labors for you. She will be at your beck and call for as long as you live but she will come at a high price to you. She will cost you one eye, one arm and a leg." Adam thought this over for a few minutes and said," What can I get for a rib?"

Court was being held where a Father bear and a Mother bear were in a legal battle for custody of their young teenage daughter. After listening to long and tedious arguments and testimonies from both sides, he asked the young bear to come to the stand and be sworn in.

She was then asked if she wanted to go live with Father Bear. "NO!" she replied, "He beats me all the time." "Then would you like to go live with Mother Bear? "NO," she beats me worse than my father does."

The judge frowned and then asked, "Is there anywhere else you could go?" "Yes," she answered, we have relatives in Chicago that I know would be happy to take me in." "And you feel like you would be safe there?" "'Yes, she said, "Everyone knows that the Chicago Bears don't beat anybody."

A carpet layer worked on installing new carpet in three rooms of a house for all of one work day. As he was finishing up with the last room, he decided he would take a smoke break, but could not find his pack of cigarettes. After searching for a few minutes, he saw a lump under the carpet near the middle of the room. After mulling this over for a few minutes, he decided that ripping up the carpet for a half empty pack of cigarettes just wasn't in his best interest.

So he took a hammer and tapped the bulge down until it was just barely noticeable. He was sure no one would ever know. His worries were allayed when the lady of the house came in a few minutes later to inspect the carpet installation in the last of the three rooms. "Very, nice," she said, "Very, very nice, I don't think I have ever seen a better job.'

"Oh, by the way, I found these cigarettes in the hallway. You must have dropped them there. Now, if I can just find my silly parakeet."

Two vultures decided to fly to Florida for a vacation and packed two bags of road kill for their flight. When they checked in at the airport, they were asked if they would like to check their bags and one responded "No, they are carrion."

Why do Women in leather dresses do strange things to men? When they encounter a pretty woman in a sleek leather dress, their pulse rate goes up, their throats get dry, they get weak at the knees and they begin to think irrationally.

Why? It reminds them of the smell of a new truck.

A psychology professor asked his class, "What kind of person can be seen to yell and scream one minute and then sit in a chair with their head down sobbing the next?" A student replied" A basketball coach."

A teacher asked two students to stay after class. She told the two boys, "Robert," she said to one of the boys, "I believe that you copied your answers from Billy's test paper yesterday." "Why do you say that?" asked Robert.

She replied, "First of all, your test average to date has been 64 and Billy's has been 96. On this test, both of you scored exactly 92 and every answer was exactly the same except one." "Well doesn't that tell you that it might be possible that I studied a little harder and did better and like you said , they were not EXACTLY the same were they?" "She said, I might agree with you except for question number 5. Bobby just wrote down, "I don't know the answer." You wrote down, "Neither do I."

A blond in the first class section of a plane put on her IPOD soon after takeoff and oblivious to all else began singing in a loud voice along with Joe Cocker "YOU ARE SO BEAUTIFUL! YOU ARE SO BEAUTIFUL!" A stewardess quickly came over to her and tapped her on the shoulder and said, "Please be silent!" She nodded and resumed, "YOU ARE SO EAUTIFUL! YOU ARE SO EAUTIFUL."

An Irish father wrote a long letter to his son who had gotten into trouble for selling illegal guns and had been sentenced to prison. He told his son how much he missed him especially now since it was time to begin turning up the acre of land where they always planted potatoes and that he had been unable to find anyone else to help him.

The son wrote back, "Dad, whatever you do, DO NOT DIG in that area. That's where I hid the guns." The very next day, the farm was swarmed with police with shovels and digging equipment. After searching all day long they were unable to find any firearms and abandoned the search.

The next day, the old farmer got another letter from his son that said simply, "Now, plant the potatoes."

An Irishman, an Englishman and a Scotsman were walking near a beach when they spotted a lamp. When they picked up a genie appeared and granted each of them a wish. The Scotsman said, "I am a fisherman and I wish that the sea would always be abundantly full of fish. No sooner said than done; the sea was teeming with fish. The Englishman said, "I would like to see a wall around all of England so that no more Scotsmen or Irishman could possibly get in. No sooner said than done; all of England was surrounded by a huge concrete wall.

The Irishman said, "Before I make my wish can you tell me a little more about that wall?" "Certainly," said the genie. "It is 500 feet tall and 50 feet thick." "Well, then" replied the Irishman, "Fill her up with water.

A nice looking Irish fellow was sadly walking alone along an old country lane when a very short and hideously ugly female leprechaun appeared. She said, "What seems to be the trouble, lad?" I lost my job and have no money," He replied. She said, "That's no problem. When you get home you will find $500,000 in your checking account." "That will be wonderful," he answered.

"If only now I will be able to convince my dear wife to return home with my two darling children. "Don't worry," she said. "When you get home they will all be waiting for you.

"Oh, thank you," He said, "How can I ever repay you?" "You can kiss me and hold me and make love to me," she said. Repulsed, but not wanting to incur her anger, he complied with her wishes. When they finished, wanting to be sure that his efforts were satisfactory, he said, "So now, all that you promised will be waiting for me at home?" She asked, "How old are you?" "Forty," he answered. She said, "Aren't ye a little old to believe in leprechauns?"

As a woman got on a bus carrying a baby wrapped in a blanket, he driver took one look at the child and said, "Geez lady, you sure got an ugly baby there. She gave him an ugly looked, ignored him and made her way to the back of the bus where she angrily sat down. The man across the aisle asked, "Was that driver being impolite to you?" She said, "Yes, he was."

"Well, then why don't you get his badge number and report him? They can't be discourteous to the public. She said, "You're right. I think I will go get it." "Good for you!" said the man. "Here, let me hold your monkey for you."

A man was driving a long distance and was growing very sleepy. As he passed through the outskirts of a small town, he decided to pull into a park and sleep for an hour or so. He did not realize that he had stopped beside a well used jogging trail. As soon as he had nodded off, a jogger tapped on his window and asked if he knew the time. He told the man, "3:30" and went back to sleep.

A little while later, another jogger knocked and asked for the time. He told the woman, "3:45" and again tried to get back to sleep. Before he could another man knocked and asked for the time. He told the man "3:50."

Then, tired of being awakened, he got a piece of paper and a pen and wrote in big block letters, "I DO NOT KNOW THE TIME", and placed it under his windshield wiper. A little bit later a jogger knocked on his window and said, "SIR, its 4:00.

A fisherman was sitting in his boat in the middle of a lake waiting on a bite when he got to wondering if he had brought along his fishing license. He got out his wallet to check and as he did dropped it into the lake. The lake was very clear and at the place he was fishing was about 20 feet deep. He watched as his wallet swayed back and forth and dropped deeper and deeper.

Then he saw a large carp grab the wallet and begin to swim away with it, then another carp snatched it away from the first and before he could move more than a foot away another carp took it away from him. It was a bad case of "carp to carp walleting."

The library at the University of South Carolina (you may place the University of your choice at this spot) burned down destroying all 20 books located there. Unfortunately 15 of them had not yet been colored.

A devout fan of the Green Bay Packers (or NFL team of your choice) finally got to Lambeau field to see a game in person. The only tickets left placed him in the nosebleed section. He did think to bring along his binoculars, but was still having difficulty watching the game.

He spotted a seat that was not occupied on the fifty yard line about four rows up. He watched it for a while and it was apparent that no one was sitting there.

So he made his way down to the seat and asked the man next to it if it was being used. "No," he said. "It's my wife's seat and she has passed away." You are welcome to sit there if you please."

He replied "Thanks!" and sat down. His curiosity got the better of him and he asked the man, "Why haven't you given the seat to a relative or a good friend?" "Oh, he replied, "They are all at the funeral."

A newly graduated police recruit was assigned to a partner and sent out on patrol. He desperately wanted to show his partner, a 20 year veteran on the force, that he was up on all the latest procedures and that he would be an asset to the team. After an hour or so of riding around with no problems evident anywhere, the recruit saw a crowd of people standing on a street corner. He told his partner to pull over.

He got out, looked around and upon seeing no valid reason for this assembly told the crowd in a loud voice, "Ok, People let's break this up! Move on please!" Everyone looked around at each other, but no one moved. "The officer said, even louder this time, "I SAID MOVE OUT!

If anyone is still standing here two minutes from now, I will place them under arrest."

The crowd reluctantly dispersed.

He sauntered back over to the patrol car, got in and asked his partner, who had not moved, "We'll looks like I handled that one ok."

"Yeah." he replied. "Those people standing around at a bus stop can be a real menace at times."

Six retired Irishmen were playing poker in O'Leary's apartment when Paddy Murphy loses $500 on a single hand, clutches his chest and drops dead at the table. Showing respect for their fallen brother, the other five continue playing standing up.

Michael O'Connor looks around the room and asks, "Oh, me boys, someone has got to tell Paddy's wife. Who will it be?" They draw straws and Paul Gallagher draws the short one. They tell him to be discreet, to be gentle and to not make a bad situation worse.

"Discreet? I'm the most discreet Irishman you'll ever meet. Discretion is me middle name. Leave it to me.

Gallagher goes over to Murphy's house and knocks on the door. Mrs. Murphy answers and asks what he wants. Gallagher declares, "Your husband just lost $500 and is afraid to come home. "Tell him to drop dead!" says Murphy's wife.

"I'll go tell him." says Gallagher.

Brenda O'Malley is home making dinner as usual when Tim Finnegan arrives at her door. "Brenda, may I come in?" he asks. "I've something to tell ya."

"Of course, you can come in, you're always welcome here Tim. "But where's my husband?" 'That's what I'm here to be telling ya, Brenda. There was an accident down at the Guinness Brewery.

"Oh, God, no!" cries Brenda. "Please don't tell me."

"I must Brenda. Your husband Shamus is dead and gone. I'm so sorry."

Finally she looks up at Tim and asks, "How did it happen, Tim?"

"It was terrible Brenda. He fell into a vat of Guinness Stout and drowned."

"Oh, my dear Jesus! But you must tell me true Tim, did he at least go quickly?"

"Well, Brenda, no. In fact he got out three times to pee."

A father is at a restaurant with his young son. He gives the boy three nickels to play with to keep him occupied until their food arrives. Suddenly, the boy starts choking and turning blue in the face. The father realizes the boy has swallowed the nickels and starts slapping him on the back. The boy coughs up two of the nickels, but keeps choking. The father panics and starts shouting for help.

A well dressed, attractive, serious looking woman in a dark business suit is sitting nearby reading a newspaper and sipping a cup of coffee. At the sound of the commotion, She looks up, puts down her coffee cup, neatly folds her paper, gets up from her seat and makes her way, unhurried, across the restaurant.

Reaching the boy, the woman carefully drops his pants, grabs the boy's testicles and starts to squeeze and twist them, gently at first and then ever so firmly. After a few seconds, the boy convulses violently and coughs up the last nickel, which the woman deftly catches in her free hand. She releases the boy, hands the father the errant nickel and returns to her seat without saying a word.

After checking his son to be sure he is ok, the father rushes over to the young woman and starts thanking her saying, "I've never seen anything like that before. It was fantastic. Are you a doctor?"

"No", the woman replied. "I'm with the IRS."

A man brings his wife to the emergency room and after a doctor examines her, he comes out to talk to the husband. He tells him, "I'm sorry, but I really don't like the looks of your wife." The husband replies, "Me either Doc, but she is a great cook and is wonderful with the kids."

Old Folks

One evening they were watching TV and George asked Betty if she would get him some ice cream. She told him she would be glad to and got up. He said, "Oh, did you want me to write you a note, honey?" "Heavens, No, I think I can remember a simple thing like getting a bowl of ice cream." He said, "Well, I wanted you to put some strawberries on the ice cream, so maybe I had better write you a note." She said, "Don't be silly," and stormed out of room. Quite a while later she returned to the room, carrying a platter of bacon and eggs. He just looked at her and said, "See, I told you I should have written you a note. You forgot the toast."

A doctor called up his 80 year old patient George and said, "I'm afraid I have some bad news and some worse news for you George." "Well," he replied, "Tell me the bad news." The doctor sighed and told him that the bad news was "You only have 24 hours to live." "My God!" said George, "What could be worse news than that?" The doctor said, "I've been trying to get in touch with you since yesterday."

An old gentleman arrived at a butcher shop just as he was it was closing on Thanksgiving eve. The old man pleaded with the butcher to let him buy a turkey telling him that he would be in great trouble with his wife if he didn't get one and that he had let it slip his mind all day.

The butcher took pity on the old fellow and let him in the shop. He went to his cooler to see what he had left since his sales had been very brisk especially on turkeys.

All he could find was one very scrawny turkey, and he took it out to the man. The old man said, "Boy, he looks pretty bad, could you please see if you have anything else?"

The butcher returned to the cooler and double checked, but could not find any other turkeys so he thought he would try to fool the old man and brought the same turkey back and said, "I found a little bit better one, but that is all I have." "The man said, "He doesn't look any better, why don't you just give me both of them?"

An old man went to a ranch while on vacation to go horseback riding. It has been many years since he had been on a horse so he asked the rancher for his most gentle horse. He told him, he had one that was a little old and its eyesight was fading, but that he was the gentlest animal on the ranch. The rancher said, "He was raised from a foal by our pastor and when he died, we bought the horse to use here on the ranch. The only problem with him is that instead of "get-up," you have to say "Thank God!" to get him to go and "AMEN!" to get him to stop."

"That shouldn't be any problem, "said the man. So in a few minutes, he was on his way. The horse proved to be very gentle and in no time he was very comfortable with the horse and soon learned that as he could increase the horse's speed by saying, "Thank God" twice and then even faster by saying it three times in a row. Soon, he was at a very fast trot and then a gallop. He then saw what looked to be a steep cliff dead ahead and the horse was headed straight for it. "Oh, my God," He said, "What was it I was supposed to say to get him to stop?"

They drew nearer and nearer to the cliff and he was in a full scale panic when he suddenly remembered and started shouting "Amen! Amen!" to the horse. The horse slid to a stop at the brink of the cliff. The man exhaled a heavy breath and said, "Whew! Thank God!"

An older couple was attending their state fair and decided to go see all of the animals that had been brought to be judged. In the cattle barn they found all of the prize bulls that he been brought to show.

The first one they came too was a magnificent Black Angus bull. A sign was posted on its pen that read "This bull mated fifty six times this past year." She poked him in the ribs and said "George, you could probably learn something from that bull. That's a little more than once a week."

He just grunted and they moved on to the next stall where they found a large Brahma bull. His sign read, "This bull mated 156 times this past year. "Maybe it would be better if you took lessons from this one," the wife said. That's three times a week. Again he grunted and they moved on.

At the next stall, they found a huge white face Hereford whose sign said, "This bull mated 365 times this past year." "Wow," said the wife.

This is the one I think you need to have as your mentor. That is once every day." This time George said, "Yeah, and I bet you it wasn't with the same old heifer every day."

An old man was seen sprawled over three seats in the rear of a movie theater by an usher. He tapped the man on the shoulder and told him, "Sir, you can't take up three seats and sleep in the theater. Please sit up or I will have to ask you to leave." The man raised his head muttered some unintelligible words and again lowered his head. The usher roused him again and said "Sir, if you don't sit up, I will have to get the manager." The man stirred again and then slumped back on the three seats.

The usher left and returned with the manager. The manager looked at the man and said, "Sir, I was just in here a little while ago and I did not see you back here. Where did you come from?" The man slowly lifted his head, groaned and said, 'From the balcony."

A painter was hired to paint the outside walls of a small white church. He finished three sides and found himself with only a half gallon of paint. He decided to just add some paint thinner rather than going back into town for more paint. He managed to add enough to complete the job and it looked as good to him as the other three walls.

A few days later he came back by the church to be paid and the pastor asked him to come around to the back wall with him.

As they rounded the corner, he saw that his paint job had not stood up and that the wall was much lighter than the other three. The painter immediately confessed his crime to the pastor who replied, "I understand my son. Sometimes the devil tempts us into such wrongful acts. Now my son, "Go, Repaint and Thin" no more."

A juggler was traveling from one town to another to meet up with the traveling circus where he worked when he was pulled over by a state policeman. As he was asking the driver for his license and registration noticed the juggler's knives laying on the front seat. He asked him what he was doing with so many knives and he explained that he was a juggler.

He said, "I use them as the grand finale of my act". The trooper said, "Ok, if you are really a juggler, let's see you juggle them." So the juggler got his knives and got out of the car. He was madly twirling them when an elderly couple drove by.

"Gosh, Margaret," said the husband," I hope we don't get stopped around here. Look what they are making you do now."

A man was eating at McDonalds when an elderly couple picked up their order and seated themselves near him. He watched as the husband cut a hamburger in half and gave one half of it to his wife. Then, he took their single order of fries and counted out half for each of them. They also only had one drink and were taking turns sipping it. The man felt badly for them and said, "I'm guessing that you are both retired." The wife said, "Yes, we are young man." He said, "I know times are tough for people these days, especially those on fixed incomes and I was wondering if you would let me buy you another hamburger and an order of fries. She said, "That's not necessary, young man, we just go 50/ 50 on everything, but thank you for asking."

He told them they were welcome and returned to his meal. He then noticed that she was not eating, just watching her husband eat. He jokingly said to her, "You'd better eat up before your food gets cold." She said, "Oh, I will. It's just Harold's turn with the teeth."

A pastor at the end of his Sunday sermon told his small town congregation that next Sunday's sermon will be on "The Sin of Lying" and that he wanted everyone to read Mark 17 before the service. The next Sunday as he began his sermon, he asked, "All of you, who read Mark 17, please raise your hand." Every hand was raised. "Ok," he said. If you will all open your bibles to Mark, you will see that there are only 16 chapters, so now let's discuss the sin of lying.

An old man and his wife had been arguing all morning and decided to go for a Sunday drive to let things cool off. As they passed a farm, they could see several sheep, some pigs and two mules. The husband could not contain himself and said, "Some of your relatives?" "Yes," she said, In-laws."

A five year old came into the den where his grandfather was seated and asked him, "Grandpa, can you make a sound like a frog?" "I don't know," he answered, "why are you asking?" The boy said, "Because,

Grandma told me that when you croaked, she would take me to Disneyland."

A gravely ill old man had been allowed to come home to spend his last few moments there. His youngest grandson came into his bedroom to say goodbye to him. His grandfather in a very weak voice asked him to come nearer. In a whisper he said, "Billy, I think your grandmother is baking some of my favorite chocolate cookies."

"I can smell them from here. I would like to taste one more of them before I die. Will you go ask Grandma for one and bring it to me?" He said, "Sure, Grandpa" and left the room. In a few minutes he came back and said, "Grandma said they were for AFTER."

An old Jewish Grandmother had her youngest grandson at the beach. He was decked out in a new red bathing outfit that she had bought for him and was playing in the sand just below her feet at the edge of the shore. All of a sudden a large wave rolled in and swept him away. She jumped up and rushed into the edge of the water but could not find him anywhere. He had been utterly and completely swallowed by the sea.

She sloshed back to the shore and fell down on her knees in the sand and began praying. "Oh, Lord, Please give me back my grandson. I promise if you do, I will be your faithful servant for the rest of my life. I will be at the synagogue for every service and I will devote my life to your works if you will only bring him back."

Just as suddenly as the first wave had appeared, another came and deposited her grandson at her feet completely unharmed. She looked at him and then looked to the skies and said, "He had a hat!"

Rednecks

YOU KNOW YOU ARE A REDNECK IF:

1. You share the recovery room with a sick cow and the bill is figured in dollars or chickens.

2. Your momma calls you up because she has a flat tire—on her house.

3. Your beer can collection is considered a tourist attraction in your town.

4. Your parakeet has learned the phrase "Open up—It's the Police"

5. You have put a clapper on your truck's headlights.

6. Your grandmother can correctly execute the sleeper hold.

7. Your favorite hunting dog has a larger tombstone than your grandfather.

8. Your pocket knife has ever been referred to as "Exhibit- A"

9. You have ever been stuck in your driveway.

10. You have used your parole officer as a reference.

11. You have ever scalped tickets after the concert is over.

12. You have ever used a toilet seat as a picture frame.

13. You have ever financed a tattoo.

14. Your neighbors started a petition because of your Christmas lights.

15. Cruise control on your truck involves fishing line, a pulley and a hook.

16. People mistakenly come into your yard thinking you are having a yard sale.

17. Your kids have ever taken a siphon hose to school for "Show and Tell."

18. Your father has ever executed the "Pull my Finger "Trick at a wedding reception.

19. You can burp and say your name at the same time.

20. Chiggers are listed as one of your top five medical concerns.

Religion

An Irish beat cop in a small New York town witnessed a rear end collision at a red light on his beat. He walks over to the car in front and sees that it is the local Rabbi Danowitz. "Rabbi, are you ok?" He asks. Yes, George, I am fine. My neck hurts a little, but I think I am fine." Do you know how fast the driver was going that ran into you?" He asks. "No, but I'm sure I gave him plenty of time to stop," the Rabbi answered. George then walks back to the second car and sees that Father O'Malley from his church is the driver. "Father O'Malley," he anxiously asks, "Are you ok?" Yes, my son, he responds. George then asks, "Do you have any idea, Father, How fast the Rabbi was going when he backed into you?"

A devout Catholic man was getting a haircut at his usual barbershop and tells the barber that he is leaving that weekend for a trip to Italy, that he will be visiting the Vatican and that he hopes to see the Pope while he is there. "How are you flying?" asks the barber. "On Air Italia," he answers. "Oh no," said Joe the barber. That is the worst airline in the world. The seats are cramped. They have lousy food and terrible service. You will not enjoy that flight.

Where are you staying?" At the Four Seasons Hotel in Rome," the man replied. "Oh no, said Joe. "We stayed there. It is horrible. They have tiny rooms, terrible food and lousy service. You will not enjoy your stay there.

And I assure you that you will not get to see the Pope unless it is with fifty thousand other people in the plaza looking up at a tiny figure on a balcony."

When the man returned from his trip, he went by the barbershop to see Joe. ""Ralph, you're back from your trip" he said as he entered the store. How was your flight over?"

Ralph said, "It was fantastic. We got bumped up to first class and were treated like kings. All the leg room you could want, an excellent meal and all we could drink. It was wonderful. "Well, how about the hotel, not good, huh?"

"No, it was great also. We were waited on hand and foot, had the most wonderful room I have ever stayed in. We could not have been treated any better." Well you didn't get to see the Pope did you?" Well it was like you said to start with. We were among a very large crowd as the Pope was conducting Mass from the balcony. But as we were standing there a man came up to my wife and me and asked us if we would like to see the Pope.

He explained to us that the Pope send him out into the crowd every time he conducts a mass to select someone for a personal audience with him."It's his way of staying in touch with people since so much of his life is isolated from the people he serves."

"So," Ralph continued, we were taken to his private quarters and enjoyed a long talk with him. "Joe asked, "What did you talk about?" "Well, the first thing he did was to lean over and look me in the eye and say, "My son, may I ask you a question? I said, "Certainly Father!" He then asked, "Where in the world did you get that terrible haircut?"

A renowned faith healing preacher was conducting a revival. At the end of the service, he asked for anyone who had a special prayer request to come forward. Occasionally, he provided hands on prayer for the healing of a body part or the improvement of an affliction. One man said to him, "Would you pray for my hearing?"

The preacher grabbed the man by both ears and issued a loud prayer. He cupped his hands over the man's ears and shouted, "Heal this man." Then he released him and asked him how his hearing was now. He said, "I don't know. It's not scheduled until next Wednesday."

Two priests decided to go to Hawaii on vacation. As soon as they had arrived and checked into their rooms, they went shopping to accomplish an idea they had discussed on the plane during their trip. They wanted to dress so that they would not be recognized as priests and be able to just mix in with all the other tourists and enjoy their time away from their parishes.

They soon were decked out in brightly colored shorts and shirts and went down to the beach to relax in the sun for a while. They both got drinks at the beach bar, rented chairs and an umbrella and set up on the beach to enjoy the beautiful weather.

Shortly after they had sat down, a drop dead gorgeous blonde wearing only her bikini bottoms approached them and as she walked by said "Hello Fathers." They both were in shock and unable to speak before she had walked on by.

After discussing the situation, they decided that they must still look like priests and went back to the beach store. This time they bought more brightly colored clothes and added hats and dark sunglasses to their attire.

Upon returning to the beach, they saw the young girl coming back down the beach and again she walked over to them and said, "Hello Fathers". This time one of them asked." Young lady, how is it that you know we are priests?" "Father," she replied, "It's me, Sister Kathleen.

A company that printed bibles interviewed a young man applying for a job as one of their door to door salesmen. He had a very bad stutter, but the manager decided to give him a chance anyway. After the first week, he was his top salesman selling an average of 12 bibles a day. His other five sales people were only averaging one or two a day. He asked him to come in so that he could ask him how he was able to sell so many bibles day after day

"We we weee—lll,' He said, I, I I riiing the dooorbbelll and when they comme to the doooor, I tell them that I, I I am se se eelling bibles and that theyyyy oooonly cost twelve dolllllars and, and fifty ceeeents. If they saaaa-y no, I sayyy, if you doooon't haaave one then, I, I, I will be glaaad to cooome in aaaaand read itt to theemm.

A redneck church was holding a week long revival that featured local musicians as part of each service. The congregation enjoyed wonderful gospel music all week long from a variety of excellent players of guitars, fiddles, drums, mandolins, banjos, and the piano and organ. Late in the week, a clarinet player took the stage and it was apparent from the beginning that he was not as proficient on that instrument as the preceding players had been on theirs.

Someone in the congregation yelled out, "Get that asshole out of here"

The music stopped and the pastor came to the pulpit. 'I cannot allow that kind of talk in the Church of God." Who said that?" No one answered. He looked at a man in the front row that often was vocal about his opinions of the church business. And said" Bobby Joe, was that you that called the clarinet player a vile name?" "No sir," he replied." It was not me"

He then looked at another likely candidate and said "Bubba, was it you that called out?" "No sir," he said. "It was not me that called that clarinet player an asshole, but since you asked, I would like to know whoever called that asshole a clarinet player in the first place."

A man came into work one Monday morning with two black eyes. One of his coworkers asked him what had happened to him. He told him that he had a little problem at church Sunday. ""Two black eyes at church?" he replied in amazement." Yeah, he said, "I was sitting behind Ms. Fitzpatrick. She is a red headed Irish woman that is, shall we say, a little big boned. When we stood to sing the first hymn, I noticed that her shirt was wedged up in her crack very badly and he slip and panties were showing. It was not a pretty sight and I was so embarrassed for her that as discreetly as possible I reached up there and pull the dress out of her crack. She immediately turned around and socked me in my left eye, turned back around and kept on singing."

"So what happened to your right eye?" He was asked. "Oh, that happened when I was putting the dress back where it was."

Three old friends were all killed in a car accident and arrived at the gates of hell together. They were met by Satin who told them that they were about to be assigned to their spot in hell for all eternity. He told the first man, "Tom, step forward." About that time the ugliest woman the men had ever seen appeared. She was about three fee six inches tall, covered in warts and had hideous teeth.

"Tom," the Devil continued, "You have sinned and this will be your wife for all eternity as your punishment" They were sent off together. He then said, Matt," Step forward. You have sinned, so now you may meet your new wife."

The second wife was uglier then the first. She was over six feet tall, covered in tattoos, body piercings, had no teeth and made continual grunting noises. They were sent off together. "Now, Don, step forward." About that time Cindy Crawford was ushered into the room.

Don could not believe his eyes. He knew that he had been no better man on earth than his two friends and was wondering what was going on here. The Devil said, "Cindy, you have sinned---

Jesus and Moses were playing golf. As they approached a 180 yard par three just over a pond, Jesus asked Moses, "What do you think Arnold Palmer would hit here?" "Probably a five iron, replied Moses. So, Jesus hit a five iron and landed about five feet short of the green into the water. Moses said, "I'll get it." He then parted the water, walked to the ball and brought it back. Jesus asked, "So, you really think Palmer could get there with a five iron?" "Moses said, "Yes, I'm pretty sure <u>HE</u> could."

So, Jesus tried the five iron again and again landed short of the green in the water. HE said, "I'll get it this time," as He started walking across the water to retrieve the ball.

Just as he was reaching the ball a foursome drove their carts up to the tee. Looking out at Jesus walking on the water back to the tee, one of them asked Moses, "Geez, who does that guy think he is, Jesus? "No," said Moses, "That guy is Jesus. He thinks he's Arnold Palme

A nun was pulled over by a state trooper. When he got to the window, he said, "Sister, I pulled you over because you were going so slowly. I wanted to see if there was some problem with your car." She said, "Oh, no, I was just trying to go the posted speed limit, 22 miles per hour. He said, "That's the route number Sister, Highway 22. The speed limit is 65."

The trooper then noticed that the nun in the passenger seat was sobbing and shaking as were the three nuns in the back seat of the car. He asked the driver if they were ok; if they were afraid of policemen. She said, "No, I think it might be because we just turned off of Highway 119."

Satan challenged St. Pete to a baseball game between the best players in Heaven and the best ones in Hell. "I would love it" said St. Pete. "But you realize that I have got all of the best players and coaches that ever played the game." "Yeah, I know," replied Satan, "But I got all the umps."

A life-long atheist was hiking on a remote trail when a ferocious bear charged out of the woods after her. She began running for her life and the bear charged after her. She ran as hard as she could but the bear soon overtook hr and slammed her to the ground.

As the bear stood over her ready to make its kill, she shouted, "Oh, God, save me!" Time stood still. The bear was frozen into inactivity and the voice of God came from the sky.

"You have been a practicing atheist all your life and now when your life is in danger you call on me? Would you like to NOW become a Christian?"

She replied, "I tell you what. If you really exist, make this bear into a Christian." "OK", was the reply. The bear stepped away from her and fell to its knees and said, "Thank You Lord for that which I am about to receive. Amen!"

SEX

The owner of a sex paraphernalia shop was visited by a friend who stopped in often. Since they were trusted friends, he asked him to watch the shop while he went to the bank. Soon after her left a woman came in and asked to see some dildos. He opened a drawer marked White—6-9 inches--$50 each. She selected one, paid him and was soon on her way. Shortly thereafter another woman came in and also asked to see his dildos. He showed her the first drawer and she asked if he didn't have anything a little larger, so he opened the next drawer marked Black—9-12 inches--$100 each. She selected one of these, paid and left.

As soon as she had left another woman entered and asked to see the largest dildos he had. He started with the White drawer and was immediately told to move on. He showed her the Black drawer and told him they were nice, but didn't they have anything larger.

He did not know all of the stock in the store so he looked in the next drawer and had started to shut it when she said. "Wait; let me see that plaid one." He told he that this was Joe's private drawer and that he would not want anything sold out of it. 'I don't care," she replied. I must have it. I will give you $500 for it.

Reluctantly, he agreed and collected her money. She exited the store with a large smile on her face just as Joe returned from the store. He said, "Sell anything?"

"Yes," his friend answered, A White dildo for $50, a Black dildo for $100 and," he laughed and added, "I got $500 for your Thermos bottle."

A man along with a dog and a pig were the sole survivors of a plane crash and had been marooned on an island for six months. The man dreamed of sex every day and had begun eyeing the pig with some interest. The only problem was that every time he got near the pig, the dog would start growling and snarling at him as it got between the pig and the man. He was a very friendly dog at all other times, but never failed to keep the man separated from the pig.

Then one day they heard an airplane approaching that was in obvious trouble with both engines on fire. It crashed nearby and he could only see one survivor. He swam out to help the woman who was hanging on for dear life to a suitcase. When he got her ashore he saw that she was a gorgeous, beautiful young woman. She thanked him profusely for saving her life and told him that she would do anything he liked to repay him.

He said with a smile, "Would you hold that dog for a few minutes?"

The Madame of a large and well know house of ill repute heard the front doorbell ring and upon answering it saw a man sitting there who had no arms and no legs. Repulsed, she said "What do YOU want?" The man replied, "Well, I rang the doorbell didn't I?"

A young man came over to home of his in-laws to be the day before his big wedding was scheduled. He had been invited by the parents for lunch. All during the meal he noticed that his bride's sister who was sitting next to him kept putting her leg against his and giving him a smile whenever he looked at her.

She was one of the most attractive women he had ever seen and was aroused by her discrete attention. Soon after the meal, the parents told him that they were taking his bride to be to pick up some last minute items and that if he would, he could keep their other daughter company while they were gone.

As soon as they left, the attention from the sister increased. She finally told him that she knew they would be gone at least an hour or two and that if he was interested, she would be in her bedroom.

He was taken quite by surprise and as soon as she had left the room, he quickly headed for the door. As he left the house he was met by the sister's family including his wife-to-be. The father said, "You have passed the "Wedding Test" young man."

"We had to know if you would be a true and loving husband to our daughter."

Moral of this story--- <u>Always</u> keep your condoms in the glove box of your car.

Two mute brothers arranged blind dates together and after they had gone to a drive-in movie and were headed to a local burger joint for something to eat, used sign language to communicate with each other.

The driver signed to his brother in the back seat, "Does it look like you might get lucky with your date?" "Yes," he answered. "How about you?" "It's looking pretty good. Do you have any condoms?" "No, I was hoping you did". The girls were watching all of the signing with great interest but did not say anything."

"I have an idea," said the brother in the back seat. "Pull up to a drug store and I will run in and get some while you drive around the block." "Great plan," said the driver as he did as instructed. When he picked up his brother, he asked, "Did you get them?"

"No, I couldn't make him understand what I wanted, so I put a twenty dollar bill on the counter and pulled it out of my pants and laid it on the counter beside the twenty. That bastard pulled out his and laid it on the counter and took my twenty."

Into an Irish pub comes Sean O. Grady, looking like he'd just been run over by a train. His arm is in a sling, his nose is broken, his face is cut and bruised and he's walking with a limp.

"What happened to you Sean?" asked the bartender.

"Jamie O'Connor and me had a fight," says Sean.

"That little O'Connor?" says the bartender. "He couldn't do that to you by himself. He must have had something in his hand."

"That he did," says Sean, "A shovel is what he had and a terrible lickin' he gave me with it.

"Well,'" says the bartender. "You should have defended yourself. Didn't you have something in your hand?"

"That I did," said Sean. "Mrs. O'Connor's breast and a thing of beauty it was; but useless in a fight."

A young girl asks her boyfriend to come over to her house to meet and have dinner with her parents. She also told him that after dinner she would like to make love to him for the first time. He was ecstatic, but he had never had sex before, so he went to the pharmacy to get some condoms.

He tells the pharmacist it is his first time and he spends an hour with him explaining all about condoms and sex. He is asked at the register if he wants a three pack, a ten pack or a family pack. Since he thinks this whole thing sounds so good, he elects to get the family pack.

That night, the boy shows up for dinner where he is quickly escorted to the dinner table and introduced to his parents. The boy offers to say grace and bows his head, a minute passes and he is still in deep prayer.

Five minutes pass and he still has his head bowed. The girlfriend leans over and whispers, "I had no idea you were so religious." He whispers back, "I had no idea your father was a pharmacist.

That's all Folks!!